Understanding the Struggle Between Natural Man vs. Spiritual Man

Robert Childress

WESTBOW
PRESS®
A DIVISION OF THOMAS NELSON
& ZONDERVAN

WestBow Press books may be ordered through booksellers or by contacting:

WestBow Press
A Division of Thomas Nelson & Zondervan
1663 Liberty Drive
Bloomington, IN 47403
www.westbowpress.com
1 (866) 928-1240

ISBN: 978-1-9736-1841-6 (sc)
ISBN: 978-1-9736-1840-9 (e)

Print information available on the last page.

WestBow Press rev. date: 02/01/2018

Contents

Preface

The struggle between the flesh and spirit of the best Christian is very real. I, myself struggled for years in my Christian life trying to find peace with God and through these struggles I have devoted myself to put in print those studies to find I can rest in the arms of Christ Jesus my Lord and it is to Him alone I give glory and honor.

God Bless. This book offers a pace of hope and rest to the struggling soul not a comfort zone to willfully sin. And it is my prayer that the reader will be inspired, encourage and challenged to find rest and peace with and in Christ Jesus now and for eternality.

Justification Defined
Roman 3:21-28

The righteousness of God is neither an attribute of God, nor the changed of character of the believer, but Jesus Christ Himself, who fully and completely met in our stead and behalf every demand of the law, and who is, by the act of God called imputation (Lev.25:50; James 2:23) made us righteous 1 Cor. 1:30).

The believer in Christ is now by grace through faith is covered or shroud under so complete and bless with righteousness from which the law from Mt. Sinai cannot find fault neither condemnation. Therefore the righteousness of God by faith of which the believer in Christ Jesus is declared justified. 2 Cor 5: 21, Rom 4:6 Roman 10:4, Phil 3:9 Rom 3:26

Robert Childress Dr. Ministry

Chapter One

Natural of Man and The Spiritual Man

Ephesians 6:12 "For we wrestle not against flesh and blood, but against principalities, against powers, against the rulers of the darkness of this world, against spiritual wickedness in high places".

To clarified the subject Natural Man and Spiritual Man..."Natural is that of human nature and the Spiritual concerns the "soul and spirit" of mankind.

But the natural man receives not the things of the Spirit of God: for they are foolishness unto him: neither can he know them, because they are spiritually discerned.

Satan is a strong enemy, so the Apostle Paul exhorts us to be strong in the Lord and to put on the armor of God. Satan knows that the flesh is weak (Mark 14:38); and that it can only be overcome by and in Christ's power. In the following you will see that it is in Christ that we can live victoriously when we realize who we are in Him and in the power of His might. Because of the Cross "the sacrifice that God provided" those that believe are seated with Christ in heavenly places far above all principalities and powers (Eph. 1:19, 23), and that this power to overcome the struggle of the natural man is in the indwelling Holy Spirit (Eph.3:14-21).

The difference between what the flesh wants and what the spiritual man needs. The war or struggle between that which is flesh and that which is spirit. It is the battle that war against the **natural man and the spiritual man**.

The natural man or the Adamic nature is among the finest of the Christian in this body even though denounced, hidden away, be that of the dieing of the old man, racing through the fancies of "being now made righteous"; it is evident at times and under circumstances well known and is brought out to surface. The

Apostle Paul stated in Romans 7:14 "O wretched man that I am! Who shall deliver me from the body of this death?" No greater words could had been clarified for the believer to understand as the Adamic nature leaps out causing confusion at times struggling within trying at best to live in the state of either sinless or in the state of perfectionism. This does not mean that we are not to strive to live a life that is pleasing unto God. There are things that we should and should not allow becoming believers in Christ. We are to cast off the old things of the Adamic nature putting on the "new man in Christ" But the point is directed by this writer that we do struggle between the flesh and the Spirit.

The nature of man (that is the fleshly minded person) seeks things in a different light to be successful. It demands full sovereignty; as it desires to attach itself with all the lusts, desires, ambitions, gratification of achievements. While the spiritual man desire to strive completely to the submission of the Holy Spirit. The motive behind the natural man is of the earth, (see, touch, taste and handle); while the spiritual man seeks by faith, growing more depended upon the Word of God, reaching forth unto the unseen yet believing through the Spirit. Total dependence upon the merit of grace and mercy of God the Father.

The natural man focuses upon all things that please self, the spiritual man seeks after and focuses upon that which pleases Christ Jesus. God never instructs us to reform the natural man (the flesh) but rather reckon it destroyed (crucified) with Christ.

> Gal 2:20 'I am crucified with Christ: nevertheless I live; yet not I, but Christ liveth in me: and the life which I now live in the flesh I live by the faith of the Son of God, who loved me, and gave himself for me."

Herein lays the struggle that many fall into such a conflict and grows into deep despair of having a desire to be perfect in the spiritual life but coming to see that the natural man is always rising in control causing doubt to one's true genuinely regeneration, (the spiritual man). And with that guilt and conviction it would be absence unless there is a Spiritual pull or motivation unto repentance. With the power of conviction and the will to obey the Lord's command there is strong evidence of reason to believe one is saved; else there would not be a struggle; as the natural man does not seek after God (ref. John 1:13 the will of the flesh). While in the natural man alone without regeneration or new birth in Christ there was never a struggle (for the spirit was dead). The outward man perish, yet the inward man is renewed day by day (II Cor. 4:16). The Spiritual man focuses on the things not seen; for the things which are seen; are temporal; but the things which are not seen are eternal (II Cor. 4:18). Faith in the spiritual man looks towards the Eternal things through the eyes of faith; while the natural man only can see what is present to the eyes that is the touch, taste and handle; or the outer appearance of religious do's and do not's.

> II Cor. 11:14 "And no marvel; for Satan himself is transformed into an angel of light".

The natural man in their quest for ambitions in promoting themselves is nothing more that the temptations that are devised by this fallen light. It is seen from the fall of Adam in Genesis chapter 3 and I John 2:16 among other places in Scriptures. John labels these natural ambitions as to the lust of the flesh, the lust of the eyes, and the pride of life. These three avenues that open up to the satanic temptations stem from the tripartite fallen nature of man, (body, soul and spirit). Thus the whole man is corrupt, depraved before they are regenerated (born again). The Apostle Paul had such religious ambitions as seen in Philippians chapter three.

> I Corinthians 15:44 "There is a natural body, and there is a spiritual body".

The deceiving fact in most religious groups today is that they are trying to improve the natural man and do not yet understand that the natural man has not been redeemed yet (Romans 8:23) but the spirit and soul of man has been through the redemption of the blood of Jesus Christ on the Cross, who having become sin for us. The Apostle Paul in Philippians 3:3 to have no confidence in the flesh and he further gave up his nature ambitions over quoting in verse 7 "But what things were gain to me, those I counted loss for Christ". Saul, before God converted him, had the pedigree in religious gratification, self justification, and righteous achievements from self. He had the very zealous ambitions in his efforts to do God's work; yet it was through the natural man. It was a form of self-righteousness. On his conversion and conviction, he counted all but lost to gain Christ; having no more confidence in the natural man but dieing to self and beginning to understand the quickening of the Spirit towards the spiritual man (which is "Christ in you the hope of glory"). In Philippians chapter 3 Paul seems to be boasting of his achievements but a closer look shows us that all his human or natural ambitions no matter how impressive cannot obtain nor earn one's salvation. Saul had the perfect credentials; parenting, born into the right nationality, inheritance, bold in his orthodoxy religion, having great zeal, and according to the law blameless (II Cor.1:9; Gal. 1:13-24). However upon his conversion all this religious history he counted as dung (waste); to win Christ and his salvation was based not on "self" but the righteousness of Christ Jesus and the Cross (the shed blood of the lamb of God) and not in any human or natural abilities of the flesh. Jesus said it clearly in John 15:5 "...without me ye can do nothing". According to Ephesians 2:1 "And you hath he quickened, who were dead in trespasses and sins". The natural man apart from the spiritual man is dead. Yet the natural man seeks after the ambitions of the flesh; or what one can gain in this life without any regards to the Eternal Life or the fear of running towards the White Throne Judgment of God.

The natural man's attitude is in the boasting of self, self-glorying without any regards to giving thanks unto the Heavenly Father for success.

The natural man thinks "what is best for me". Their self motivation is in survival, self-interest, self-satisfying. Their drive is in staying alive and well out of self efforts and being productively is their primary concern. Out of these two basic principles lays the motivation and behavior. It is a short term satisfaction not looking at the long term Eternal or end result or consequence of any danger to their actions. As if they capture the moment at any cost without the regard of others involved.

What the natural man seeks after _____

The natural man seeks after the physical attention as in body building, physical attractions, health and wealth; which are needful in the right priority. There is the emotional element "what makes me feel good apart from the Spirit?" This discover as to what the natural man invests time, talents and money in. Being filled with "self confidence" that is "What I do is okay" without any convictions. Being made right in one's own eyes; under their own opinion and seeking after self-justification as to why I do the things I do. This self-confidence of motivation is the means in the natural man struggles to survival to reach their highest potentials and self-satisfying pleasure in life.

There are three sources that make up the way the natural man thinks that makes one feel successful and they use these for their purpose of existing they are 1. Position 2. Power 3. Possession. Break these walls for success and the natural man breaks apart in despair. Losing the controlling force of position, power or possession and it destroys the natural man's ability to be successful as their foundation is shaken. They base these three things in determining their self worth and if intruded upon it engages all kinds of mental breakdowns in depressions, feelings of rejections, resentments and other factors that leads into some form of religion to feel good or an addiction of drugs and alcohol. The natural man comes into the state of being a victim of what God has created with the feelings of rejection from self ambitions. With this kind of attitude it opens up the reaction of the fallen nature of man in vengeance, jealousness, rebellion and thus leading into all kinds of self reconciling themselves in spiritual delusions and doctrines of devils .A false sense of security that governs the flesh. The age long question that is asked is; "What must I do to be saved"? It is not what must I do; but the acceptance and receiving what Christ Jesus did on the Cross.

Where it all began

It all began in the Garden of Eden. Ecclesiastes 1:9 "The thing that hath been, it is that which shall be; and that which is done is that which shall be done: and there is no new thing under the sun". The same deceiving devices of temptation that Adam and Eve faced are the same today. Adam did not just lose his innocence position with the Father but also he picks upon himself the natural man's traits. Not only did he disobey the Lord's command that brought the whole world into the state of sin, but because of that "his eyes were opened" and the feeling of separation because of sin began the religious cycle of self ambitions to be righteous through works; "as he made himself aprons to cover up his nakedness". Eve was deceived by the serpent towards the natural abilities of ambitions and lust of the flesh.

In fact when the walls of security were broken, Adam's innocent position and power was broken and he hid himself from the fellowship of his Creator. His trust in God became questionable. This very idea of the natural man came into place when he sewed fig leaves together to cover his error or sin. It was a direct failure of trusting God that brought about a self-righteous act to cover the guilt.

Cain in Genesis 4:3 "brought of the fruit of the ground an offering unto the Lord". Genesis 6:5 "And God saw that the wickedness of man was great in the earth and every imagination of the thoughts of his heart was only evil continually". In the tower of Babel in Genesis 11:4 we can see the natural man seeking humanist ambitions of pride building up; "And they said, 'Go to, let us build us a city and a tower, whose top may reach unto heaven, and let us make a name, lest we be scattered abroad upon the face of the whole earth". Abram sought the Lord through faith. Lot had the natural man in view as in Genesis 13:10 "And Lot lifted up his eyes, and beheld all the plain of Jordan, that it was well watered". While the spiritual man depends on trusting God by faith; the natural man follows that which can be seen, touched and tasted. Faith is: that which comes from the Word of God resting or trusting in His promise; while the natural man sees that which is visible to the eyes the spiritual man sees the invisible.

The natural man seeks ways through "what is best for self". It is the old "I" trick of Lucifer in Isaiah fourteenth chapter (The deceiving I will's). What works best to suit "me".

Their self motivation is in their survival, self-interest, self-satisfying and self serving to be acceptable (it is their power to achieve). These fig leaves were an act of releasing the guilt and being made self-satisfying rejecting the real need of man; and that which is acceptable unto God the Father. Cain is next in line. Religious "fig leaves" is the ambitions and attitude of the natural man in being made self acceptable unto the Heavenly Father. Man's greatest need is not the outward or natural acceptance but rather and inward spiritual need of acceptance being acceptable or reconciled back to their Creator and the Scriptures declares the only way back is to repent of sins and receive that one and only sacrifice given once for all to declare man justified; being made righteous in the sight of God (Hebrews 9:11-15). And that righteousness is found in receiving the gift of salvation by the means of the Blood of Jesus Christ that was shed in our behalf and for our healing (Isaiah 53; John 3:16).

What the natural man does not understand is how another can remove the guilt of sin and breaking down the wall of separation from us from Holy God. Yet the natural man seeks after trying to please the flesh and does not see what the spiritual man needs. The redemption plan of salvation is the working of God the Father through the vessel of Jesus Christ becoming flesh and taking our place to die for the sins of the whole world. This came not by the will or forethought of man's device but before the foundation of the world; God had a plan for man's redemption. Seen in the promise seed that should come (Genesis 3:15).

From the time of Adam's fall man has sought after the means of a pure heart before God through the means of sacrifices, baptisms, and even religious good works. Somewhat to balance out good from bad. These things might add to the

Eternal weight of rewards but only one offering was made acceptable to reconcile man to God and that is the blood of the Lord Jesus Christ on the Cross.

Facts, not feelings are the focus on one's salvation. We might not at time feel saved, but we are not saved according to our feelings but according to the promise of God's Word; "faith cometh by hearing and hearing by the Word of God". Just as the deceiving lie that Satan threw at Eve, "can we rest on the fact of God's Word?" Is there any doubt to His Word on the saving of our souls? The one simple emotional factor that controls the human heart is **trust**. Any doubt defiles that pure trust of faith, and it does not matter what we say it cannot change it. Is our faith based on facts of the written Word of God or feelings? "This saith the Lord" or feelings. One person said "I see what the Scriptures say but I cannot accept that as a fact". Neither did Eve; as she listened to the serpent and created doubt and begin to take roots.

The steps of a good man is ordered by the Lord; so if the natural man seeks after ambitions and has attitudes let them be control by the Lord's will not merited after personal natural self pleasing, self efforts of the natural man.

There are Two Natures of the Believer

There are two natures that dwell within the believer; they are different one from the other. While one seeks after the things of this world (flesh) {even in a good sense such as prosperity, position and pleasure}; the other seeks after that which is above {the spiritual things, the eternal things}. The natural man will only see the temporal things that will fade away; but the spiritual man seeks about the things of the Spirit that shall remain eternal in Heaven.

When a person is born again by the Spirit of God, they do not lose the "old Adamic, sin nature" but is given a "new nature" or "new birth" has taken resident within. The old is to be reckon "dead" but how much it is reckon "dead" it is still there. Paul reckon it to be that of this death (Romans 7:24; also see Galatians 2:20). Being made a parker of the divine nature has to do with maturing into the Christ-likeness being regenerated in the thoughts, minds and heart of every believer. Born again yes, but the outward character and the will of man is daily being transformed into the complete Holiness of God and that is a life long process that is controlled only as we surrender more and more unto the Lord Jesus; (II Peter 3:18) that teaches us to grow in grace.

There is nothing holy or good about the flesh. It is carnal, self-seeking, self-justifying, self-glorying and very much sinful. Sinful in both commission and omission of the things we allow. This is the struggle the Apostle Paul had and is still the same struggle we face today; between the natural and the Spiritual part of man. The natural man apart from the Spiritual is works of the flesh and has no room to justify itself. On the other side; the new nature, being born again has nothing in itself that is neither unholy nor unacceptable with God through repentance and faith in the Lord Jesus Christ. The new nature is received by grace through faith and it is the God's nature, and it can not be anything but holy, acceptable and pure in the sight of Holy God as John 3:6 teaches; "that which is born of the flesh is flesh, and that which is born of the Spirit is Spirit". Therefore we as believers should see the difference; however most only understands this as being perfect or sinless in the Christian life.

Did Paul struggle with the flesh and the Spirit? Romans 7:18 "For I know that in me (that is, in my flesh,) dwelleth no good thing: for to will is present with me; but how to perform that which is good I find not". Certainly he did and he gave an honest answer of the source of the struggle in verse 20 "...sin that dwelleth in me". Isaiah 64:6 "But we are all as an unclean thing, and all our righteousness are as filthy rags; and we all do fade as a leaf; and our iniquities, like the wind, have taken us away". Isaiah 17:5 "Thus saith the Lord; Cursed be the man that trusteth in man, and maketh flesh his arm, and whose heart departeth from the Lord"; verse 7. This can be seen two ways; trust in the strength of others in position and power; or trusting in one's own abilities. "Blessed is the man that trusteth in the Lord, and whose hope the Lord is". If we struggle with the idea of working this flesh into a state of perfectionism to the point of being acceptable unto the Holy and Righteous God are we truly trusting in Jesus or our abilities to being made justified in His site?

Many have tried but in vain to keep the law of God but failed miserably. Are we being made righteous apart from true repentance and faith towards God?

The Scripture clearly state that all our righteousness are as filthy rags? Psalms 39:5 b"...verily every man at his best state is altogether vanity".

Romans 3:10 "As it is written, There is none righteous, no, not one".

Every honest believer will; experience a struggle between the flesh (the natural man) and the Spirit. Galatians 5:17 "For the flesh lusteth against the Spirit, and the Spirit against the flesh: and these are contrary the one to the other: so that ye cannot do the things that ye would". The cry of the struggle Paul face is seen as the source for peace is in Romans 7:25 "I thank God through Jesus our Lord". What was the source that he could thank God? Romans 4:25 "Who (Jesus) was delivered for our offences, and raised again for our justification. That being justified by faith, we have peace with God through our Lord Jesus Christ". It is no more the struggle within our self the "natural man" but rather the "Spiritual man" Christ in us that justifies us and the resurrection of Christ Jesus is the witness that God accepted that Sacrifice for our sins once and for all (Hebrews 10:10) "By the which will we are sanctified (set apart) through the offering of the body of Jesus Christ once for all". The struggle has ended for Paul in chapter 8 and this verse in Romans 3:20-25 becomes clear:

> "Therefore by the deeds of the law there shall no flesh be justified in his sight: for by the law is the knowledge of sin". (The law reveals sin; and the guilt of sin).

> "But now the righteousness of God without the law is manifested, being witnessed by the law and the prophets; Even the righteousness of God which is by faith of Jesus Christ unto all them that believe: for there is no difference: For all have sinned, and come short of the glory of God; Being justified freely by His grace through the redemption that is in Christ Jesus:

> "Whom God hath set forth through faith in His blood, to declare His righteousness for the remission of sins that are past, through the forbearance of God".

The law is likening to a mirror it reveals sin in us but has no source to remove the sin or imperfection. It makes no difference how hard we struggle in the natural man to please God; it is impossible without the guiding and conviction of the Holy Spirit. For we have all come short to the glory of God. But that glory is "Christ in you"; For He is 'the Life' (Colossians 1:27).

There is a great need among many people to belong to the family of God. I say to the family of God as many are not in church as they feel uncomfortable belonging to a group that are control by a list of do's and do not's. They judge each other by the acts they do. Moreover, if you don't live up to their standard doctrines and decrees you are not one among them.

The Christian life is just as the name implies (life); and that life is given by none other than Jesus Christ and the source is the death burial and resurrection of our Lord.

The Christian life is given by and through the strength and power of God and by any other means is not acceptable.

John 10:1 Verily, verily, I say unto you, He that entereth not by the door into the sheepfold, but climbeth up some other way, the same is a thief and a robber.

If all your desire is how well you perform as a Christian to be acceptable in the site of God you have failed to see the Grace given unto freely.

> Rom 8:1 There is therefore now no condemnation to them which are in Christ Jesus, who walk not after the flesh, but after the Spirit.

> Rom 8:2 For the law of the Spirit of life in Christ Jesus hath made me free from the law of sin and death.

> Rom 8:3 For what the law could not do, in that it was weak through the flesh, God sending his own Son in the likeness of sinful flesh, and for sin, condemned sin in the flesh:

> Rom 8:4 That the righteousness of the law might be fulfilled in us, who walk not after the flesh, but after the Spirit.

> Rom 8:5 For they that are after the flesh do mind the things of the flesh; but they that are after the Spirit the things of the Spirit.

> Rom 8:6 For to be carnally minded is death; but to be spiritually minded is life and peace.

Rom 8:7 Because the carnal mind is enmity against God: for it is not subject to the law of God, neither indeed can be.

Rom 8:8 So then they that are in the flesh cannot please God.

There is no glory in the flesh. The outward working of the flesh that is to justify ourselves; neither to base ourselves in a righteous manner towards God. For all our righteousness is useless in the eyes of God. It is through the blood of Jesus Christ the Lamb of God that takes away the sin of the world.

Thereby all glory is due Him that died and is alive forever more. It is the spirit of man not the flesh that matters. And that spirit in man is Born from above as seen in John 3

> Joh 3:5 Jesus answered, Verily, verily, I say unto thee, Except a man be born of water and of the Spirit, he cannot enter into the kingdom of God.

> Joh 3:6 That which is born of the flesh is flesh; and that which is born of the Spirit is spirit.

> Joh 3:7 Marvel not that I said unto thee, Ye must be born again.

> Joh 3:8 The wind bloweth where it listeth, and thou hearest the sound thereof, but canst not tell whence it cometh, and whither it goeth: so is every one that is born of the Spirit.

The Apostle Paul is a good example of having a fleshly show of wisdom being zealous in keeping the Law; (and I call the list of do's and do not's).

Php 3:4 Though I might also have confidence in the flesh. If any other man thinketh that he hath whereof he might trust in the flesh, I more:

Php 3:5 Circumcised the eighth day, of the stock of Israel, of the tribe of Benjamin, an Hebrew of the Hebrews; as touching the law, a Pharisee;

Php 3:6 Concerning zeal, persecuting the church; touching the righteousness which is in the law, blameless.

Php 3:7 But what things were gain to me, those I counted loss for Christ.

Php 3:8 Yea doubtless, and I count all things but loss for the excellency of the knowledge of Christ Jesus my Lord: for whom I have suffered the loss of all things, and do count them but dung, that I may win Christ,

Php 3:9 And be found in him, not having mine own righteousness, which is of the law, but that which is through the faith of Christ, the righteousness which is of God by faith:

Php 3:10 That I may know him, and the power of his resurrection, and the fellowship of his sufferings, being made conformable unto his death;

Paul under the name Saul was a very zealous religious person. What he was doing according to the law was blameless. "thy shall have no other gods before me". These whom he had persecuted for following Christ he according to law was doing the will of God.

But Saul was stopped dead in his tracks of religion to find "It is Christ in you the hope of glory".

Eph 2:4 But God, who is rich in mercy, for his great love wherewith he loved us,

Eph 2:5 Even when we were dead in sins, hath quickened us together with Christ, (by grace ye are saved;)

Eph 2:6 And hath raised us up together, and made us sit together in heavenly places in Christ Jesus:

Eph 2:7 That in the ages to come he might shew the exceeding riches of his grace in his kindness toward us through Christ Jesus.

Eph 2:8 For by grace are ye saved through faith; and that not of yourselves: it is the gift of God:

Eph 2:9 Not of works, lest any man should boast.

Eph 2:10 For we are his workmanship, created in Christ Jesus unto good works, which God hath before ordained that we should walk in them.

God will not judge us on how well we performed; but how well we trusted and receive the One (His Son Jesus).

The Christian Life is Christ Jesus.......

The new and living way

Not trusting in the flesh but allowing the Holy Spirit to work through us without condemnation.

Salvation is a gift according to John 3:16

It is by grace through faith

Cannot be merited or earned on human behavior but accepted by the heart. Trusting in the one that died on the Cross for your sin.

The Christian Life is simply "Christ is the Life"
The giver of Life
The keeper of that Life

I John 3:9 "Whosoever is born of God doth not commit sin; for his seed remaineth in him; and he cannot sin, because he is born of God". The Scripture refers to the new nature (The Spirit nature). This divine nature is God's nature (the seed of God) and God's seed is from God's who is Holy, Righteous and cannot sin; if so could God become sin through the implantation of the flesh of mankind?

I Peter 1:23 "Being born again, not of corruptible seed, but of incorruptible, by the word of God, which liveth and abideth for ever".

When a believer has been repentant and born again what does that person receive? Does the believer receive an incorruptible seed? Can it become corrupt?

Jude 24 "Now unto him that is able to keep you from falling and to present you faultless before the presence of His Glory with exceeding joy". II Thessalonians 3:3 "But the Lord is faithful, who shall stablish you, and keep you from evil".

The question must be asked; do we as Christian's sin? To be honest yes and the Scriptures declare that the struggle with the natural man and the spiritual man is sin. I John 1:6-10 "If we say that we have fellowship with him, and walk in darkness, we lie, and do not the truth: But if we walk in the light, as he is in the light, we have fellowship one with another and the blood of Jesus Christ his Son cleanseth us from all sin. If we say that we have no sin, we deceive ourselves, and the truth is not in us. If we confess our sins, he is faithful and just to forgive us our sins, and to cleanse us from all unrighteousness. If we say that we have not sinned, we make him a liar, and his word is not in us".

These verses presuppose that a Christian can and does sin, also they instruct us what to do when we do sin.

I John 2:1 "My little children, these things write I unto you, that ye sin not. And if any man sin, we have an advocate with the Father, Jesus

Christ the righteous". Much of the New Testament exhorts believers not to sin, but to live holy, separated lives before God and men.

Sanctification

On the other side of this doctrine of entire sanctification is the teaching of "fallen from grace" which is in most cases miss-understood. As well seen in the above lesson it is Christ Jesus through unmerited favor He has saved us; implanted the incorruptible seed of God in us and that he is able to keep us. Either salvation is a gift of God as the Scriptures speaks or it is a salvation of works. (see Eph. 2:4-9)

"But God, who is rich in mercy, for His great love wherewith he loved us, even when we were dead in sins, hath quickened us together with Christ, (by grace ye are saved). And hath raised us up together, and made us sit together in heavenly places in Christ Jesus. That in the ages to come he might shew the exceeding riches of his grace in the kindness through Christ Jesus, For by grace are ye saved through faith; and not of yourselves: it is the gift of God" Not of works, lest any man should boast"

If salvation was of works:
1. What kind of work is required?
2. How long must one work to attain peace with God?
3. What if you failed to succeed?
4. Who is to judge the struggle of the performance of that work?
5. What happens to the definition "grace" as being an unmerited favor with God?

This grace, mercy and kindness is an act from God during the time when we were dead in trespasses and sins. The spiritual man is redeemed not by an act or merited of his own but by the single act of God's love (John 3:16) For God so loved the world...." Out from God's own Divine character produced the agape love as He provided a way of redemption of which none other could produce from the natural man. No ambition, no attitude of reformation could man rescue himself from the "old Adamic nature". The teaching "falling from grace" is not that of the possibility of losing one's salvation (Gal.5:4 "Christ is become of no effect unto you, whosoever of you are justified by the law; ye are fallen from grace". The interpretation here is that you have misunderstood the message and purpose of Christ and God's grace. However Ephesians 1:13 states: "In whom ye also trusted, after that ye heard the word of truth, the gospel of your salvation; in whom that ye believed, ye were sealed with that holy Spirit of promise, which is the earnest of our inheritance until the redemption of the purchased possession, unto the praise of his glory". The doctrine of "eternal security" is taught in Scriptures (John 10:28,29, Romans 8:35-39, Ephesians 1:13-14, Ephesians 4:30, Philippians 1:6, I Peter 1:5, Jude 24). In Christ and through repentance and faith in Christ Jesus; what sin could possibly cause one to fall out of the grace of God? Where were we when God demonstrated His love towards us? At what point in sin did we fall out? How many sins did Jesus pay for on the cross? Was the cross the finished sacrifice for sin? To whom did Jesus die for; He became sin for whom? Just suppose one could lose their salvation; how does one lose it; by not performing good works or the lack thereof? Is not this then "a salvation based of the natural man's effort to gain Eternal Life?

Is there a Way of Total Victory in the Christian Life as we struggle between the natural and the Spiritual?

> Romans 6:11 "Likewise reckon (to regard as being consider) ye also yourselves to be dead indeed unto sin, but alive unto God through Jesus Christ our Lord".

The Scriptures does not promise to get rid of (completely) the "old nature", but rather, to gain the victory over it through faith in the Lord Jesus Christ.

I Corinthians 15:55-58 "O death, where is thy sting? O grave, where is thy victory? The sting of death is sin: and the strength of sin is the law. But thanks be to God which giveth us the victory through our Lord Jesus Christ". Therefore, my beloved brethren, be ye stedfast, unmoveable, always abounding in the work of the Lord, forasmuch as ye know that your labour is not in vain in the Lord".

Beginning in the Garden of Eden after the fall we see God at work making coats of skin to cloth Adam and Eve. It was from Genesis through the New Testament that the sacrifice of another in shedding of blood what was required for atonement to cover up the guilt of sin.

The struggle between the natural man and the spiritual man and trying to reach a sinless perfect state of sanctification has put a tremendous mental and spiritual burden on those who claim a second blessing. That is a fear of sinning and thus falling from grace. But "God has not given us the spirit of fear; but of power, and of love, and of a sound mind" II Timothy 1:7. This writer knows the struggle between trying to live the Christian life and falling until the Holy Spirit opened the Scriptures of stop trying and began to trust. It is Christ Jesus and Him alone that we have a complete assurance of our salvation and even the victory over sin. As Christ Jesus through the blood of the cross has removed sin, redeemed man and salvation is of His working it out:

> John 6:63 "It is the spirit that quickeneth (made alive): the flesh (natural) profiteth nothing: the words that I speak unto you, they are spirit, and they are life". While being honest, we do sin and is witnessed by Scriptures, we are to reach forward and reckon this body dead to sin, and seek the things that please God.

Real victory comes through power, not the power from one self (that of the flesh) but the power of Christ who dwells within us.

> I John 4:4 "Ye are of God, little children, and have overcome them: because greater is He that is in you, than he that is in the world".

> Colossians 2:10 "And ye are complete in him, which is the head of ALL principality and power".

> Matthew 28:18 "And Jesus came and spake unto them, saying, All power given unto me in heaven and in earth".

There is no power greater than He; and He along has power over ALL things:

> Philippians 3:10 "That I may know him, and the power of His resurrection, and the fellowship of his suffering, being made conformable unto his death".

Here the Apostle Paul (during this time was referring to his former life 'as Saul) was very zealous in obeying the law; working out of the natural man and was in my view a very dedicated natural man trying to please God through "holy ambitions and attitude" but verse 7 sums it up "But what things were gain to me, those I counted loss for Christ". The main objective here is seen in verse 3 "...worship God in the spirit and rejoice in Christ Jesus, and have no confidence in the flesh". Here the struggle has ended. Philippians 1:6 "Being confident of this very thing, that he which hath begun a good work in you will perform it until the day of Jesus Christ".

I Corinthians 1:18 "For the preaching of the cross to them that perish foolishness; but unto us which are saved it is the power of God".

Ephesians 1:4-23 Paul, an apostle of Jesus Christ by the will of God, to the saints which are at Ephesus, and to the faithful in Christ Jesus: Grace *be* to you, and peace, from God our Father, and *from* the Lord Jesus Christ.

Blessed *be* the God and Father of our Lord Jesus Christ, who hath blessed us with all spiritual blessings in heavenly *places* in Christ:

According as he hath chosen us in him before the foundation of the World, that we should be holy and without blame before him in love: Having predestinated us unto the adoption of children by Jesus Christ to himself, according to the good pleasure of his will, To the praise of the glory of his grace, wherein he hath made us accepted in the beloved.

In whom we have redemption through his blood, the forgiveness of sins, according to the riches of his grace; Wherein he hath abounded toward us in all wisdom and prudence; having made known unto us the mystery of his will, according to his good pleasure which he hath purposed in himself:

That in the dispensation of the fulness of times he might gather together in one all things in Christ, both which are in heaven, and which are on earth; *even* in him:

In whom also we have obtained an inheritance, being predestinated according to the purpose of him who worketh all things after the counsel of his own will:

That we should be to the praise of his glory, who first trusted in Christ.

In whom ye also *trusted,* after that ye heard the word of truth, the gospel of your salvation: in whom also after that ye believed, ye were sealed with that holy Spirit of promise,

Which is the earnest of our inheritance until the redemption of the Purchased possession, unto the praise of his glory.

Wherefore I also, after I heard of your faith in the Lord Jesus, and love unto all the saints, Cease not to give thanks for you, making mention of you in my prayers;

That the God of our Lord Jesus Christ, the Father of glory, may give unto you the spirit of wisdom and revelation in the knowledge of him:

The eyes of your understanding being enlightened; that ye may know what is the hope of his calling, and what the riches of the glory of his inheritance in the saints, And what *is* the exceeding greatness of his power to us-ward who believe, according to the working of his mighty power, Which he wrought in Christ, when he raised him from the dead, and set *him* at his own right hand in the heavenly *places,* Far above all principality, and power, and might, and dominion, and every name that is named, not only in this world, but also in that which is to come:

And hath put all *things* under his feet, and gave him *to be* the head over all *things* to the church, Which is his body, the fulness of him that filleth all in all.

> God enables us to live victoriously over sin, Satan, self, and the world through FAITH I John 5:4-5 "For whatsoever is born of God overcometh the world: and this is the victory that overcometh the world, even our faith. Who is he that overcometh the world, but he that believeth that Jesus is the Son of God?"

Simple put it is Christ Jesus and HIS RIGHTEOUSNESS that we can have a perfect standing with the Heavenly Father.

> Romans 5:1 "Therefore being justified by faith, we have peace with God through our Lord Jesus Christ".

The natural man outside the repentance and faith of Christ Jesus can never be justified because the only ground for justification towards God is Christ Jesus: Romans 4:25 "Who was delivered for our offenses, and raised again for our justification".

> Romans 5:19 "It was by this one man (Jesus)....by the obedience of one shall many be made righteous".

Any type of reformation, religion, set of "good deeds"; neither any motivation of the ambitions of the natural man can appease God.

> II Corinthians 5:21 "For he hath made him to be sin for us, who knew no sin; that we might be made the righteousness of God in him".

This was Israel's mistake thinking that it was out of the works of the natural man to gain salvation.

> Romans 10:2-4 "For I bear them record that they have a zeal of God, but not according to knowledge. For they being ignorant of God's righteousness, and going about to establish their own righteousness, have not submitted themselves unto the righteousness of God. For Christ is the end of the law for righteousness to everyone that believeth".

While this might seem as though the believer can live any way they choose; however there is a greater restraint and that is the one in us after we are saved (the Holy Spirit).

> Hebrews 12:6-8 "For whom the Lord loveth he chasteneth, and scorgeth every son whom he receiveth,

If ye endure chastening, God dealeth with you as with sons; for what son is he whom the father chasteneth not?
But if ye be without chastisement, whereof all are partakers, then are ye bastards, and not sons".

> Galatians 5:1 "Stand fast therefore in the liberty wherein Christ hath made us free, and be not entangled again with the yoke of bondage".

> Galatians 5:13 "For brethren, ye have been called unto liberty; only use not liberty for an occasion to the flesh, but by love serve one another".

It is because of the repentant heart and brokenness of sin that we are drawn to Christ by the Holy Spirit; and it gives us the liberty to be made free in Christ; but this freedom is in experiencing the love of God and walking in fellowship with

Him and in the spiritual man. It is the constraining element that Paul speaks of in II Cornithians 5:14 "For the love of Christ constraineth us; because we thus judge, that if one died for all, then were all dead. And that he died for all, that they which live should not henceforth live unto themselves, but unto him which died for them, and rose again". If the former life of sin does not shame us; has the new life in Christ really changed your spirit? It is of this attitude of the spiritual man that over rides the natural man to cause one to seek after the love of God, the fellowship with God. Not that it will improve the natural man but it will increase the maturity of the spiritual man. John 14:15 "If you love me, keep my commandments". You will thank God and love the Lord Jesus in a way to seek after him with a true and pure heart. Not that we shall be perfect but following; pressing forward for that mark increasing our faith and devotion towards Him that loved us first. Real lasting power to overcome sin is through faith which comes through hearing the word of God and simply believing God's word putting into practice towards our daily life. That is applying daily that which we have heard from Scriptures. This Victory comes through love for God that shed abroad in our hearts by the Holy Spirit (Romans 5:5). We love Him because He first loved us (I John 4:9-13; 17-19) Our love for God motivates us to live for Him and others. True salvation changes our "want to's". We release the natural man and are no longer dependant on the self motivation, self-ambitions or self-willed; but on a greater and that is a love for him motivation, (I John 5:3; II John 6; Romans 7:22).

> "For I delight in the law of God after the inward man". While the natural man seeks to please themselves; the spiritual man seeks to please Christ and others (I John 3:23-24) "And this is his commandment, That we should believe on the name of his Son Jesus Christ, and love one another, as he gave us commandment. And he that keepeth his commandment dwelleth in him, and he in him. And hereby we know that he abideth in us, by the Spirit which he hath given us".

The victory to overcome sin comes through with a sound mind. That is a heart and mind set that will discipline and give direction. It is a direction of faith and our faith is increased unto the spiritual man through studying of the Scriptures. Our mind is the battlefield where the issues of life are decided. Our walk in this struggle between the natural man and the spiritual is "whom do we allow to direct our decisions in life. Are we being lead of the Spirit? It is the mind (the choices) we make that reckons we are dead to sin and alive unto God.

Romans 6:11 "For in that he (Jesus) died, he died unto sin once; but in that he liveth, he liveth unto God.

When we got saved, through repentance and faith towards God; the sin should had so broken our spirit so that we no longer desire; lust or seek after the natural man with its ambitions, attitudes or the lusts of the "old man". The motivation should had changed; and we no longer seeking the things that pleases the flesh but to seeking after the things that pleases the Lord Jesus Christ and to bring Him honor and glory.

Romans 6:16-18 "For sin shall not have dominion over you: for ye are not under the law, but under grace.What then? shall we sin, because we are not under the law, but under grace? God forbid. Know ye not, that to whom ye yield yourselves servants to obey, his servants ye are to whom ye obey; whether of sin unto death, or of obedience unto righteousness? But God be thanked, that ye were the servants of sin, but ye have obeyed from the heart that form of doctrine which was delivered you. Being then made free from sin, ye became the servants of righteousness."

It is important in this struggle to yield yourself to the one that you have committed yourself to obey. This is not the motivation to praise the natural man but rather give honor and glory unto the one that gave you life (Jesus Christ).

Also those that are saved having a conviction over sin in John 16:7-8 "Nevertheless I tell you the truth; It is expedient for you that I go away: for if I go not away, the Comforter will not come unto you; but if I depart, I will send him unto you.

And when he is come, he will reprove the world of sin, and of righteousness, and of judgment". The Holy Spirit that has been given us upon receiving Jesus Christ through repentance is the key factor that guides us to the making right or wrong decisions in our life. It is our mind that must be transformed from carnality. Romans 8:7 unto the spiritual man;. Romans 12:2.

"And be not conformed to this world: but be ye transformed by the renewing of your mind, that ye may prove what is that good, and acceptable, and perfect, will of God."

Ephesians 4:23 "And be renewed in the spirit of your mind".

A building is only as solid as its foundation. That foundation that believers has is Christ Jesus. He is "the life" and our purpose and reason for living. Everything we are and do must fit liken to a puzzle to see the whole picture. All of our goals in life are built on the solid foundation of Christ which is the real and lasting foundation. Otherwise we are building on the faulty foundation such as wealth, health, and these things that brings a temporal sense of security and success in life. The natural man has but only one foundation and that is "flesh is flesh" as seen in John 3. All that is of the natural man will cease. But the things of the spiritual man begin at the Cross of Christ and should be part of that motivation that works for the good towards all those that seek after the spiritual man.

I Corinthians 2:14 "But the natural man receiveth not the things of the Spirit of God: for they are foolishness unto him: neither can he know *them*, because they are spiritually discerned".

The natural man and some immature Christians are influenced by their own passions or desires (called lusts). How much influence do your own desires have on your life? Are they based on the natural ambitions to survive or have we reckon the natural man dead in Christ that through Him we can run the race of the greater goals in life; the Eternal Things. Our goals should be to let God's desires be ours. And this friend takes a life time to accomplish.

The application to this chapter is don't be so focus on the negative temporal corrupt nature of man, but rather to focus on the positive position that after you receive Jesus Christ and the free forgiveness of sins through the blood of Jesus Christ we can have peace with God through our Lord Jesus Christ. Yes, we shall struggle in this life time with the old nature as well as with the spiritual nature. But if we are so focus on our failures we shall never see the work Christ Jesus is doing and that is changing us from glory unto glory until at last changed into the glory of Christ Himself.

Chapter Two

The Struggle With Perfectionism

Galatians 3:2-3 "This only would I learn of you, Received ye the Spirit by the works of the law, or by the hearing of faith?"

Are ye so foolish? Having begun in the Spirit, are ye now made perfect by the flesh?"

There is in the struggle among Christians the idea of perfectionism. Scriptural growth of perfection is a level of maturity in which we have grown in the grace and knowledge of the Lord Jesus Christ. **But never do we reach the standard of a sinless perfection;** that is in this body of flesh (the natural man) be that of thought, deed either in commission of sins or omissions of things we should do. Holiness that is of God comes through the Lord Jesus Christ by faith just as well as the initial beginning of our salvation that is receiving Jesus Christ as our personal Savior. Holiness is just like our justification; it is a gift of God. He alone through the finished work of the Cross imputed unto those that believe the righteousness require of God. It is received and lived by faith, and is a matter of devotion and desire towards a relationship with Christ Jesus. Holiness does not depend on our performances (works) but on the faith of the one that is faithful (Jesus Christ) in His Perfect Performance.

There are many names for the "so called" counterfeit theology of "Christian Perfection", 'the Higher Life', or Deeper Life' even labeled 'the Spirit filled life". Biblical understanding of perfectionism is being matured into the faith that comes through hearing and applying the principles of God's Word to our life. Maturity in the Christian Life is again through faith in Christ, submitting more and more of ourselves (the natural man) unto His will of the impartation of the character of Christ by the indwelling Holy Spirit that is well able to give us the victory to live a life over the bondage of sin. The Apostle Paul stated in Galatians 2:19-21 "For I through the law am dead to the law, that I might live unto God. I am crucified with Christ: nevertheless I live; yet not I but Christ liveth in me: and the life I now live in the flesh I live by the faith of the Son of God, who loved me, and gave himself for me. I do not frustrate the grace of God: for if righteousness come by the law, then Christ is dead in vain". We take justification as an action from God when we received Jesus into our heart faith. Perfection or maturity in Christ is the same objective as seen in Philippians 1:11 "Being filled with the fruits of righteousness, which are by Jesus Christ, unto the glory and praise of God". It is simply Christ in you the hope of glory. The mature fellowship with God is a gift received and lived by submission and faith; it is a matter of relationship not something gained or earned. The whole relationship with the Heavenly Father is depended upon the righteousness and performance of the Lord Jesus Christ through faith and not of us. Rewards yes, but not for salvation. While we are to strive in pursuit of the excellence of Christ, yet we find at times the struggle to live up in perfect performance. But thanks be unto Christ that performs the exact Holiness and Righteousness of the Heavenly Father. Coming short of His glory however weak the gap is filled with the righteousness of Christ.

What if the faith of some is overthrown? What if sin over takes one that believe but for a moment? Just a bad thought? II Timothy 2:19 "Nevertheless the foundation of God standeth sure, having this seal, The Lord knoweth them that are his...." If perfection is built on self-glorification is the working of our salvation; this struggle will always be present in the natural man; but if salvation is totally and depended upon the shed blood of Jesus Christ and that true repentance and faith is in the Lord Jesus Christ then that salvation is built upon a sure foundation which is Christ the solid rock of which one stands. It is unshakeable, sure and steadfast. Jude 4 "Now unto him that is able to keep you from falling and to present you faultless before the presence of his glory with exceeding joy".

While at times it is a struggle; yet we can claim victory through Christ and press forward to the mark of the high calling of God in gratitude of love towards Him because of God accepting us in His Son of Righteous. It becomes a love driven passion that constraints us to follow Christ rather than a guilt or fear to obey a group of commandments or law; as Jesus said "If you love me, keep my commandments". Not through fear but love. And should we fall along the way the grace of God is sufficient enough to carry us forward to the finished line. Ephesians 2:5-6 "Even when we were dead in sins, hath quickened us together with Christ, (by grace ye are saved;) | <<note here: (times past and time future|. And hath raised us up together,

and made us sit together in heavenly places in Christ Jesus". It was the Holy Spirit that quickened us (gave life) and it is in Christ sealed unto the day of redemption that we are (present) seated. Even though we see the "now" as present tense; God sees the "now" as the future tense. The finished product of the work of redemption through the shed blood of Jesus Christ (Eph 2:6), While this might appear to be an uncontrolled walk with God; "a do as you please walk; yet the factor that constraints us is not in fear of performing but rather submitting the natural man over unto the Spirit becoming a vessel for His workmanship created in Christ Jesus. We love Him because He loved us first. While the best of honest Christians seek after to live in a manner to pleasing and obeying the commands of God it is out of love and gratitude to Him for His great love. Yet there are those that try to serve God in a way to be accepted by Him base on their performance. They are fearful in continuing straining to make themselves acceptable to God by comparing themselves and measuring themselves among themselves in rules, deeds of performing and accomplishments. The concept of this kind of theology is that their "God" is never satisfied and the illustration they present is a God that demands more and more; as one that is never please no matter how well the performance. They illustrate their God as a demanding tyrant who requires perfect performances and if that demand is not met He is ready to pour out Divine Wrath upon them. They present our Heavenly Father of Divine Grace; not willing for any man to perish as a Judge that has no tolerance for imperfection and at the slightest failure to live up to perfection ready to smash you down under condemnation and guilt. They put character before faith, works before trust, accomplishments before receiving, performance before worship. This drives the sinner that has a yearning for God; but with this God they present there is no way to match up to the performances required; because that is in this body of sin we cry like Paul "O wretched man that I am! Who shall deliver me from the body of this death" Romans 7:24. While the fear of God is the beginning to approach God, it is the grace of God that captives one. If one is held over a burning flame by a ten link chain; how many links has to break for the person to fall into the fire? When one breaks one part of the law of God; it is all broken.

According to James 2:10: "For whosoever shall keep the whole law, and yet offend in one point, he is guilty of all". Spiritual pride, boasting, jealousness among the few things not to mention the sin of omission; he that knows to do good and does it not; how are we ever to come to the state of reaching perfection or sinless state in this vile body? II Corinthians 10:12 "For we dare not make ourselves of the number, or compare ourselves with some that commend themselves: but they measuring themselves by themselves, and comparing themselves among themselves, are not wise". The Scriptures has already declared; "There is none righteous, no, not one" Romans 3:10.

The Law teaches us the knowledge of sin and the need for salvation. God provided the source for our salvation in due time sending His Son Jesus to give us salvation through the work of the Cross. He became sin for us. God's righteousness can not be based on the natural man's ability to live up to His perfect and Holy Character. To begin; we all come under the Adam's nature (the fall), "For as by one man's disobedience many were made sinners" Romans 5:19. Therefore salvation must be received by faith as a GIFT made possible by Christ's shed blood on the Cross. If one man could speak today of this fact of the operation that took place on the Cross it would be Barabbas in Matthew 27:26 as he was the guilty one and condemned but Christ took his place and he was set free. The choice was made and Barabbas was released and they crucified Jesus. The innocent one became the guilty one. Perfectionism makes God's love towards man something to earn rather than to accept freely offered, freely received. Taking away the unconditional, unmerited favor of the meaning of grace and adding to salvation if you can earn, keep and obey; making the blood of the atonement for sin as a down payment but you must carry the note. This would reduce Christianity to a set of impossible rules and would transform "Good News" into Bad News" as the natural man given the right situation can not improve neither reform itself to measure up to the perfection that is in Holy God the Father. Romans 5:8-10 "But God commeneth his love toward us, in that while we were yet sinners, Christ died for us." (Note: "yet sinners; God didn't wait until we were better, improved, work things out to better the natural man); but His unconditional love was demonstrated while we were still ungodly freely giving whosoever wills a spiritual nature; by calling upon Jesus Christ to save us.

While Adam lost much; yet in Christ Jesus much more is given. Much more then, being now justified (present tense, carried with the past tense in justifying) by His blood; we shall be saved from wrath through him. For if, when we were enemies, we were reconciled to God (how?) by the death of His Son, much more, being reconciled, we shall be saved by (whom?) his life. Verse 11 "... we have now (present tense) received (past tense) the atonement (or at- one- ment). One with Christ Jesus.

How is this proven?

If Jesus died on the Cross for all our sins; and if the atonement for our sins was completed (and it was in Christ); we have now the victory as seen in the resurrection of Christ Romans 4:25 "Who was delivered for our offenses, and raised again for our justification".

While most perfectionists will not honestly admit it, we all have among us the natural man that hold to evil desires that we cannot deny, be they of thoughts or acts. Indeed it is a struggle to resist and it is a battlefield that wars between the flesh and the Spirit. While we might not engage in any sexual immorality, drunkenness or witchcraft yet is there any self-willed ambitions, envy, strife, jealousness among us? What about any doubts as Romans 14:23 points out "whatsoever is not of faith is sin". Proverbs 6:16-17 "These six things doth the Lord hate: yea, seven are an abomination unto him: A proud look, a lying tongue, and hands that shed innocent blood". As innocent as it might be when a faithful devoted Christian gets so worked up in the blessings of God; it is easy to begin to develop a proud look at the progress in the work of the Lord. This proud look can be seen in the attitude towards others; that young convert that has to grow in grace to reach their position in knowledge of the study of Scriptures. God's grace reaches and holds up that least one without respect of persons; those that have just been born again (the babe in Christ) are just as in relationship with God as those that have been in relationship with Christ for years whom are well learned in Scriptures. Our maturity in Christ can be in the natural ambitions to succeed that we commend ourselves rather than allowing the Spirit of God to lift us up as chosen vessels for His Service. The pressure the Apostle Paul had cause him to do that which he didn't approve and that was in boasting to show forth his authority in apostleship to those in Corinth; II Corinthians 12:11 "I am become a fool in glorying; ye have compelled me: for I ought to have been commended of you: for in nothing am I behind the very chiefest apostles, though I be nothing". He was writing of the revelation about when he had been caught up into paradise of which he kept to himself but because they had questioned his authority he became boastful about such things and he revealed it to them in a letter. Earlier in the letter in chapter 10:17-18 he writes "But he that glorieth, let him glory in the Lord. For not he that commendeth himself is approved, but whom the Lord commendeth". The real test in boasting is not found in "how great we become" but how "great He is". It is Christ working in you that brings God the Father Glory, Praise and Honor. True boasting is found in Christ that is in you creating in you the workmanship as seen in I Corinthians 1:5 "That in everything ye are enriched by him, in all utterance, and in all knowledge", Ephesians 2:8-9 "For by grace ye are saved through faith; and that not of yourselves: it is the gift of God: not of works. Lest any man should boast. For we are his workmanship, created in Christ Jesus unto good works, which God hath before ordained that we should walk in them".

The natural man seeks after the ambition of perfectionism to please his ego; but the spiritual man is Christ and His seed pleases that which the Father requires. It is the Christ in you the hope of glory as it is written in John 6:63 "It is the Spirit that quickened the flesh profiteth nothing". In fact there is no boasting of the natural man's ability to come to the Father except by and through Jesus Christ John 6:65 "Therefore said I unto you, that no man can come unto me, except it were given unto him of my Father". As carnal minded as Peter was in Matthew 16:17 when ask by Christ to His disciples who He was Peter answer He was the Christ, the Son of the living God; Jesus answered; for flesh and blood hath not revealed it unto thee; but my Father which is in Heaven. We take for granted and give ourselves credit for understanding the mysteries of an Invisible but yet so Great and Powerful Eternal Father in Heaven; but it is of the Holy Spirit that illuminates the Scriptures unto us so that we can understand any thoughts of an Eternal God. The whole key to spiritual understanding of spiritual truths is depending upon the Spirit of God to unveil the mysteries of Himself John 16:13, "Howbeit when he, the Spirit of truth, is come, he will guide you into all truth..."

The Real Struggle Towards Perfectionism

The real struggle towards perfectionism is the fact: that in this human body we cannot completely attain unto that perfection. And that is to perform to the exactness of perfection that the Law of God requires. This is from the very moment that we struggle to begin unto the very last requirement that the Law of God requires. Take the Apostle Paul for example in Romans 7:9-13 " For I was alive without the law once: but when the commandment came, sin revived, and I died. And the commandment, which was ordained to life, I found to be unto death. For sin, taking occasion by the commandment, deceived me, and by it slew me. Wherefore the law is holy, and the commandment holy, and just, and good".

The declaration of Holy God has declared all our righteousness are as filthy rags (Isaiah 64:6). The New Testament in Romans 3:10 declare "There is none righteous, no not none".

> Ephesians 2:1 "And you hath he quickened, who were dead in trespasses and sins". Take a soul that is dead in trespasses and sins, the beginning

point to work out perfection is being with "one dead in sins". Job asked the question in Job 14:4 "Who can bring a clean thing out of an unclean? Not one". There is no life in the natural man other than this physical life. The spiritual man is dead in sins until the Spirit of God quickens that soul Job 15:14-16 "What is man, that he should be clean? And he which is born of a woman, that he should be righteous? Behold, he putteth no trust in his saints; ye, the heavens are not clean in his sight. How much more abominable and filthy is man, which drinketh iniquity like water?" Romans 5:18-21 "Therefore as by the offence of one judgment came upon all men to condemnation; even so by the righteousness of one the free gift came upon all men unto justification of life. For as by one mans disobedience many were made sinners, so by the obedience of one many be made righteous. Moreover the law entered, that the offences might abound. But where sin abounded, grace did much more abound: That as sin hath reigned unto death, even so might grace reign through righteousness unto eternal life by Jesus Christ our Lord". The natural man is born into a darken state of being. Because of the inherited transgression of Adam; therefore the natural man is in darkness. Those that have received Jesus Christ; it is He whom proclaimed, "I am the light of the world". Ephesian 5:8 "For ye were sometime darkness, but now are ye light in the Lord, walk as children of light". The source of light is the Lord; not within the natural man. We are the vessel that carries the fuel. Not the fuel. Outside of the Light we are in total darkness. The natural man stands totally depraved of light being a metaphor of understanding the real man. That is the man created in the image of God found in Genesis therefore it is of the nature of the natural man to build themselves up; that is to justify themselves, to seek as Cain the self-righteous ego acts of religion. There is some lacking in the natural man that seeks to fill up the gap that is in the conscious to worship "something" outside of him self. Mankind was created to Worship their Creator. Created to fellowship and to commune with but because of the fall of Adam man ended up in total darkness and has ran from their Creator. But in and through Christ He reconciled man back to the Creator. Jesus brought back that perfect light; the light that illuminates God's Divine order. Often the writer hears about those that receive Jesus Christ into their hearts as liken to a great load of guilt being removed and the Scriptures become alive that is to understanding of them. The veil of darkness is removed and their understanding being opened so that they can understand them. This is that light. And Great is that Light that takes away the darkness. The natural man does not will for this light as it will reveal the depravity in man John 3:19-21 "And this is the condemnation, that light is come into the world, and men loved darkness rather than light, because their deeds are evil. For every one that doeth evil hateth the light, neither cometh to the light, lest his deeds should be reproved. But he that doeth truth cometh to the light that his deeds may be made manifest, that they are wrought in God". In fact this darkness so blinds the natural man that they are hostile towards God and flees from the presence of God or hides in the case of Adam in Genesis three. Adam hid from the presence of the Lord. Romans 8:6-8 "For to be carnally minded is death; but to be spiritually minded is life and peace. Because the carnal mind is enmity against God: for it is not subject to the law of God, neither indeed can be. So then they that are in the flesh cannot please God".

II Corinthians 4:3-4 "But if our gospel be hid, it is hid to them that are lost: In whom the god of this world hath blinded the minds of them which believe not, lest the light of the glorious gospel of Christ, who is the image of God, should shine unto them".

Verse 6 "For God, who commanded the light to shine out of darkness, hath shined in our hearts, to give the light of the knowledge of the glory of God in the face of Jesus Christ".

Only until the natural man comes to the place of seeing all the good deeds, efforts, self-exaltation, self-glorification and any other thing of the natural ambitions or egos of man has failed; then repentance and faith towards God can he come to understand the righteousness required of God is in one man Jesus Christ THE RIGHTEOUS ONE. We in the natural cannot produce that which is required of God as our dependency rest on and in the Lord Jesus then and only then can we be standing in Christ perfect. II Peter 5:10-11 "But the God of all grace, who hath called us unto his eternal glory by Christ Jesus, after that ye have suffered a while, make you perfect, stablish, strengthen, settle you. To him be glory and dominion for ever and ever, Amen"

> Colossians 2:13"And you, being dead in your sins and uncircumcision of your flesh, hath he quickened together with him, having forgiven you all trespasses;"

Not only was Jesus raised from the dead; we are raised with Him in faith and in complete glorification through Him as seen in Romans 8:30 "...whom he justified, them he also glorified".

Chapter Three

Learning to Trust

The Scriptures calls love the greatest virtue (I Corinthians 13:13). One of the Greek words is agape"; that has the expression in the act of God's love towards unworthy mankind. It is for above any type of definition of love as other definitions is "Eros" which is a physical love and "Philia" which refers to the warmth, closeness and affection experienced in a deep friendship. Agape is the Supreme love of God; out of His Divine Character shown in Christ when He died for the ungodly. It is a love that reaches beyond the normal limits, even to the point of seeking from our enemies the good within them. This type of love is the "fruit" of the Spirit and can only be produced by the Spirit and the nature of God. It is commanded to have this same type of love one for another even as Christ also loved the church and gave himself for it. Agape has to do with the mind set; and not just a mere feeling that is produced by the natural man. History has proven that the natural man cannot agape their enemies. It is beyond our natural inclinations and emotions. The natural man is only able to love those that love and his kind to them but the Spiritual man can love not love; beyond those that don't love and is not kind back. Be kind to those that are kind...etc.

Breaking down the barriers of the natural man unto the leadership or guidance to the Spiritual man involves this kind of love. Learning to trust; begins with sharing the emotional intimacy with another of our personal thoughts and feelings. Exchanging private thoughts and feelings with a trusted friend leads to this kind of peace.

The real need for self-esteem is seen in this agape kind of friendship. Love fulfills our basic need for self-esteem, self-image that leads and supports our human identity. Ultimately it brings out the real need of the human; not of the natural man alone but greater the spiritual man in its worth and value. To lack this is to self-destruct. While the natural man judges on the basis of secular criteria; that is the physical attractiveness, wealth, worth, power and position; the spiritual man commends one's worth on the basis of that which is Spirit. "I am worth because of the value God's sacrifice has place on me". "I am valued because Jesus died for me". When the natural man falls short and their world (that is their self-image) has been crushed their emotional feelings are lost. They lose and see no value in their self-identity, having no value, worth, feel they are not loved and the bottom of this thought is in the fact they do not love themselves. A feeling of rejection, apart of any real lasting hope, and therefore raises the signs of depression, anxiety, anger, and frustration takes root.

How we feel about oneself is the driving force behind our thoughts and actions. The real struggle between the natural man and the spiritual man is learning to trust. First; trusting oneself to agree that we are sinners in need of A Savior that loves us. It is coming to the point of laying aside anything of the natural man far as "our own abilities" surveying "our natural ambitions" and surrendering oneself to the crucifying of our natural man in total dependency of allowing the Holy Spirit to quicken or making alive in us the spiritual man. And secondly; it is trusting God who is able to save and to keep us; even though we fall short of His glory in the flesh. That gap is now complete in Christ and God is willing to take us "just as we are" trusting not in the natural man but depended upon the Cross of Christ that through His shed blood has redeemed us and because He lives (raised from the dead) we too can rest assured in that we are hidden in Christ and Christ in us. Bonded together in so great of love that it will reach far into that which we could never attain.

Some struggle with the inability to let go of the natural man and trust God in surrendering unto Him alone. Just as a person hanging on to a limb that is fixing to break to catch hold of a rope to pull them into safety. It has been engraved in our spirit since childhood to be good, perform well and if we fail we are worthless and of no value. One factor that the natural man has is fear and we are fearful of things or persons we can not trust. And certainly afraid to accept to the idea of surrendering unto God; afraid that if we do not do well He will beat us down with a rod of His wrath. The human body produces chemicals which arouse our defenses in time of danger or fear; and our minds and spirit quickens that pace. While the Scripture declares the fear of the Lord is the beginning of wisdom (Psalms 111:10); it is the love of Christ that draws us unto salvation. But the natural man hesitates to let go and trust the Lord in His goodness. Some have the gut-level concept of God; they may think they are surrendering unto God in an unpredictable and fearful fate, an all-powerful monster who is ready and willing to display His wrath if one steps out of line. Many see the spiritual man as in a life that is miserable that has no "fun" without any freedom to enjoy life. For is this: to those that truly accepted the spiritual life has witness it is the most restful and peaceful life filled with rewarding moments of perfect peace. It is no longer dependency upon the natural man but rather the spiritual man connected and controlled under the leadership of the Holy Spirit.

> Matthew 11:28-30 "Come unto me, all ye that labor and are heavy laden, and I will give you rest". Take my yoke upon you, and learn of me; I am meek and lowly in heart: and ye shall find ret unto your souls. For my yoke is easy, and my burden is light".

These Scripture certainly does not contain any fear to surrender but they are a call to rest. Rest from your own labor in the flesh; (the natural man); and beginning a new life in the spiritual man leaving the results up to Jesus Christ the one that made it possible to be at peace with the Father; and He is the only true and lasting peace.

With any emotionally healthy person, there is enough original sin and selfishness to insure a continue struggle in full surrendering their will in complete trust unto God. It is because of a distorted concept of God in asking them to do what they cannot do and never will be able in the natural state of man. Yes, God hates sin, but the other side of the coin God loves the sinner enough to have sent His Son to save them through a sacrifice of Himself on the Cross. John 3:16 is the greatest love verse in the Bible. It is the very heart of God's compassion for the sinner. The Father's Divine Love for Fallen Man. God is not willing for any man to perish II Peter 3:9. In fact God's love is demonstrated in offering salvation unto any that call upon Him and trust in His Son Jesus Christ for the redemption of their soul. To trust Jesus Christ is to surrender all the effort of the natural man in appeasing God and placing full trust and confidence in the One and only means of salvation. And that is in the finished work of the Cross in the shedding of the blood of Christ that was offered up as the final and complete sacrifice for sins (Hebrews 10:10).

I admit it is a hard step to trust in another after through years of failure or broken relationships with friends and family to trust another. Many have trusted someone only to learn to be unfair, unpredictable, and undependable. The painful memories and experiences that some have had; placing our confidence in someone just to be scattered so strong that now they are call to trust anyone enough to surrender oneself to another. All the feelings from childhood rejections, resentments, abuse and abandonment surrounds so many that the sub-conscious that places a barrier to ever trust, respect or even love again. But it is these kinds of people that God will reveal His love towards those. It is learning to trust in the fact that God's Word can be trustworthy. That God keeps His promises and that He will never fail; in fact He will keep His Word above His name. Forever thy Word is settled in Heaven.

Love God, love self and others to the point that we no longer struggle with the flesh but count it dung that we might live unto God the author and finisher of our faith:

Chapter Four

"RIGHTEOUSNESS"

The Battle or Struggle Over The Flesh Is Won In Christ Jesus
ROMANS 3:21

RIGHTEOUSNESS: *Is God's Standard of Perfection. - (Deuteronomy 32:4)*
As you read God's commandments in Exodus 20:1-20 and Christ's Sermon on the Mount in Matthew 5-7, you will see that God's standard of right is absolute PERFECTION. In fact, Matthew 5:48 says:

> "BE YE THERFORE <u>PERFECT</u>, <u>EVEN AS</u> YOUR FATHER WHICH IS
> IN HEAVEN IS <u>PERFECT</u>."

Absolute perfection is *"Holiness"* and only God possesses holiness. The Bible says *God is Holy* (Isaiah 6:3 and Isaiah 57:15); but according to Isaiah 64:6:

> *MAN'S RIGHTEOUSNESS IS AS FILTHY RAGS IN THE SIGHT OF
> GOD* As we turn our attention to the book of Romans we find these
> same truths taught there in more detail. Romans 1:18 through 3:20
> basically teaches two doctrines:

1. God must judge and condemn the sinner because He (God) is Holy and His justice demands it!
Even in society, we cannot let people get away with breaking the law. There must be justice. So it is with God.

37

Romans 1:18 says: *"FOR THE <u>WRATH OF GOD</u> IS REVEALED FROM HEAVEN <u>AGAINST ALL</u> UNGODLINESS AND <u>UNRIGHTEOUSNESS</u> OF MEN WHO HOLD THE TRUTH IN UNRIGHTEOUSNESS."* (Also see Romans 2:12, 16)

The second doctrine taught in Romans 1:18-3:20 is:

2: Every person is a sinner!

There is no sense in denying it. We must all admit we've done things wrong. The Bible says so!

Romans 3:9 - *". . . THEY ARE ALL UNDER SIN."*

Romans 3:19 - *". . . <u>EVERY </u>MOUTH MAY BE STOPPED, AND <u>ALL</u> THE WORLD MAY BECOME GUILTY BEFORE GOD."*

Romans 3:20 - *". . . THERE SHALL <u>NO</u> FLESH BE JUSTIFIED IN HIS (God's) SIGHT."*

Romans 3:23 – *". . . <u>ALL</u> HAVE SINNED, AND COME SHORT OF THE GLORY OF GOD."*

Therefore; since God is holy and must judge the sinner, and since every person is a sinner we can mankind has a problem. With respect to this problem, Paul now reveals the solution to the dilemma that man is in. The solution is in the *"GOSPEL"* which was given to Paul by God - Romans 1:16; 2:16.

In Romans 3:21, Paul starts to unfold God's solution: ***"BUT NOW THE RIGHTEOUSNESS OF GOD WITHOUT THE LAW IS***

MANIFESTED BEING WITNESSED BY THE LAW AND THE PROPHETS."

"BUT" - This begins the great solution to man's sin problem. Man is a sinner but . . .

"NOW" - Indicates that the problem has been resolved and that the solution is being revealed to mankind for the first time.

"THE RIGHTEOUSNESS OF GOD IS MANIFESTED"

- This does not mean that God's righteousness was not known before. It means God's standard of right (the perfection of God) is now being made available to mankind by the gospel.

God has given to man His *holy laws,* but man was not able to keep them. Some people hope they will get to heaven by keeping the "Ten Commandments," but the point of Romans 3:19,20 is that if people would read those laws and be honest with themselves and God, *"EVERY MOUTH"* would be stopped and each person would have to acknowledge that they have broken God's laws. In fact, the reason God gave the "Law" was to point out to man his sinful condition and his need of a Savior which is the Lord Jesus Christ.

The problem is that man lacks the righteousness that God requires for entrance into heaven. But now, that righteousness is made available to man--from a source outside of himself. God's righteousness is being offered to mankind as a gift.

PRACTICAL POINT:

Since it is *GOD'S STANDARD OF PERFECTION* that is required for entrance into heaven, then our works cannot save us. In fact, our righteousness is not a part of the solution here at all. The scriptures point us to Jesus Christ and *His Righteousness.*

Another thing, since we are all sinners and our righteousness is as filthy rags, therefore our works cannot save. In fact they will only condemn us!

Chapter Five

"IMPUTATION"

IMPUTATION: *Is God's Righteousness Credited To One's Account.*

The word *"Imputation"* (or *"Impute"*) is not used in Romans 3:22. It is actually used in Romans chapter four, but the word *"UPON"* in Romans 3:22 convey the same thought (See Romans 4:3). The word *"Impute"* is an accounting term which means *"to credit to one's account."* For instance, suppose my bank account is short the necessary funds required for paying my debts. A person who loves me--and has the money--can deposit the amount necessary into my bank account which will keep me out of jail.

THE RIGHTEOUSNESS OF GOD IS UNTO ALL AND UPON ALL THEM THAT BELIEVE.

Since man **"COMES SHORT"** and cannot make himself righteous, righteousness will have to be given to him from God, otherwise there is no hope for man. This is exactly what Romans 5:17 says:

RIGHTEOUSNESS IS A GIFT FROM GOD

This God-given *righteousness* is available to man **"BY THE FAITH OF JESUS CHRIST"** according to Romans 3:22. That is to say, the righteousness of God is available to man because of the faithfulness of Jesus Christ. God is not giving out *His righteousness* as a reward to us because of our faithful service to Him. God is giving out *His righteousness* as a gift to us because of Christ's faithful service to Him. Jesus Christ always did the will of His Father, even when it came time to give up His life and die on the cross for our sins. The following verses confirm that it's Christ's faithfulness and not ours that counts with God when the subject is our salvation:

Ephesians 3:12 - Teaches that our access to God is by Christ's Faithfulness.

Philippians 3:9 - Says it is not my righteousness, but through Christ's righteousness and my faith in Him, that saves me.

Coming back to Romans 3:22, there are two important phrases to take note of:

#1. ***"UNTO ALL"*** - *This speaks of an Unlimited provision!*

God's righteousness is available to *everyone*. This is great news and again the following verses will confirm this wonderful news:

I Timothy 2:4 - ***"GOD OUR SAVIOUR WHO WILL HAVE ALL MEN TO BE SAVED, AND TO COME UNTO THE KNOWLEDGE OF THE TRUTH."***

I Timothy 4:10 - ***". . . BECAUSE WE TRUST IN THE LIVING GOD, WHO IS THE SAVIOUR OF ALL MEN, SPECIALLY OF THOSE THAT BELIEVE."***

I Timothy 1:15 - ***"...CHRIST CAME TO SAVE SINERS..."*** "Compare this with Romans 3:23 which says, ***". . . ALL HAVE SINNED . . ."***

NOTE: The provision of the cross was not always declared ***"UNTO ALL."*** In times past, it was limited to Israel (Isaiah 53:4-8 & Matthew 26:28). However, Romans 3:21 begins with ***"BUT NOW,"*** indicating a change and that the provision is now available to ***ALL***.

Both Jews and Gentiles ..."The whosoever"

The other important phrase in Romans 3:22 is this:

#2. *"UPON ALL THEM THAT BELIEVE"*

- This speaks of a Limited Application!

While God's righteousness is available to everyone, it is *imputed only* to those who believe. God in his great wisdom has chosen to credit *His righteousness* <u>only</u> to the account of those who choose to trust in Him.

> Romans 1:16 - *". . . THE GOSPEL OF THE CHRIST. . . IS THE POWER OF GOD UNTO SALVATION TO EVERYONE THAT <u>BELIEVETH</u>. . ."*

> Romans 4:3 - *". . . ABRAHAM <u>BELIEVED</u> GOD, AND IT WAS COUNTED UNTO HIM FOR RIGHTEOUSNESS."*

> Romans 4:23, 24 - *"NOW IT WAS NOT WRITTEN FOR HIS SAKE ALONE, THAT IT WAS IMPUTED TO HIM; BUT FOR US ALSO, TO WHOM IT SHALL BE IMPUTED, IF WE <u>BELIEVE</u> ON HIM THAT RAISED UP JESUS OUR LORD FROM THE DEAD."*

> I Corthinians 1:21 - *". . . IT PLEASED GOD TO SAVE THEM THAT <u>BELIEVE</u>."*

To illustrate what we have learned so far, let's say a certain man became extremely ill of a disease. He became so ill that he lost his job and with it his health insurance. Afterwards he discovers there is an operation that can cure him and without it he will die. However, having lost his job and insurance, he cannot afford the operation.

Then one day he reads in the newspaper about a very rich person who advertises that he will deposit into anyone's bank account the amount of all medical expenses for anyone who is in such a predicament. If this man will believe what he has read and receives this offer, he will live. But if he pays no attention to this provision and has the attitude that he will take care of himself, in his helplessness he will die.

PRACTICAL POINT:

The illustration may be fictitious but the truth of Scripture is not. The Lord Jesus Christ was faithful. He lived without ever sinning. He died for our sins. The provision has been made for everyone, but His righteousness is given only to those who believe, and thereby receive it.

Since Jesus Christ paid for all sins, and since it is *His righteousness* that God sees applied to my account the moment I believe in Christ, then I am secure because *His righteousness* will never fail although there will be times mine will.

Does imputed righteousness mean God makes me righteous?

Chapter Six

Understanding the Grace of God

Romans 3:24 **GRACE:** *Is The Unmerited Favor of God.*

Throughout Scriptures"Grace" is so much of a characteristic of God (like His love), that human words do not adequately express its meaning; as God's grace is above human understanding.

Romans 3:24 begins with: ***"BEING JUSTIFIED FREELY BY HIS GRACE"***

Some have defined *"Grace"* as *"Undeserved Mercy"*, and this is true. However, all mercy is undeserved; that's the meaning of mercy. **GRACE** is more than mercy. Mercy gets a criminal off the hook and out of jail, but **GRACE** pays the debt of the criminal and sets him free to enjoy the good life.

When we say that **GRACE** is *"Unmerited Favor"*, we are saying that this kind of favor <u>cannot</u> be earned. It's not just that you don't have to earn it. The fact is you <u>cannot</u> earn it. Since we are all sinners, there is nothing that we can do to gain God's favor. Even if you did good works continuously from here on out, and sacrificed all your time to help others, and did great and wonderful things twenty-four hours a day for the rest of your life to please God, God still would <u>not</u> accept you or your efforts because He is Holy and you are still a sinner. You cannot work off your sins.

God's salvation is not merited, it is a *GIFT* of God! – as seen in: Ephesians 2:8, 9. The word for **"GRACE"** (in the Greek) is *"Charis."* The word for **"GIFT"** (in the Greek) is *"Charisma."* It is easily seen that the very root meaning of the word **GRACE** is **GIFT**.

Romans 11:6 is a verse that clearly contrasts **"WORKS"** with **"GRACE."** It does that because they are exact opposites. A gift is something given freely, but work is something that you do to earn a wage. Romans 6:23 tells us what wages we have coming to us:

> *"FOR THE WAGES OF SIN IS DEATH, BUT THE GIFT OF GOD IS ETERNAL LIFE, THROUGH JESUS CHRIST OUR LORD."*

We really don't want what our sins have earned for us. Rather we want the gift that comes from God through Christ.

Since we began to study Romans 3:21-24, we have seen that God's righteousness has been made available to all of mankind today, but it is only imputed to those who believe. Then God, upon that faith, justifies or declares the sinner righteous. Now we learn that all of this is done *"FREELY BY HIS GRACE."* What a wonderful God we have!

Ephesians 3:1-5 teaches us that God's message of **GRACE** was first revealed to Paul. It was through the Apostle Paul that God's Word of **GRACE** was preached to the Gentiles.

Galatians 1:13-16 gives testimony that God's **GRACE** was what changed Paul from being the number one enemy of Christ into Christ's number one preacher among the Gentiles.

I Timothy 1:11-16 explains why God used Paul for this job of making His **GRACE** known. It was because Paul's conversion is the pattern of grace. Paul deserved the most severe punishment of hell, but by the grace of God he was saved and given the right (as all believers have today), *to sit with Christ in heavenly places* - (see Ephesians 2:6).

We have said: "Mercy gets the criminal off the hook, but grace pays his debt". Romans 3:24 goes on to tell us that the reason God is free to deal with mankind today in **GRACE** is because of what Jesus Christ accomplished for us on the Cross. The Lord Jesus Christ paid our debt of sin and, in receiving Him, we are set free to enjoy God's love and to live in His favor! He was and is the sacrifice for sin once and for all. (Hebrews 10:10 ref.)

PRACTICAL POINT:

Everything required for my Salvation has been supplied by God. Salvation is the work of God in my behalf. Now, to get that point through our stubborn thick human heads, we are told that justification is *unmerited* and *undeserved* on our part. On the other hand, it is given *freely* to us on God's part. It could not be made any clearer. Salvation comes to us, <u>not</u> on the basis of works, but on the basis of a free gift from God by grace through faith.

Since I am now in God's favor apart from any good works of my own, then-- if I happen to do a bad deed-- it does no change God's attitude toward me.

Before you jump to any conclusion, please understand; this does not mean that a believer is free to go out and continue sinning. Contrary to popular opinion--but in accordance with Scripture--as a Believer dwells upon this *grace* of God in which he now stands, it will motivate him to do good works! – see Titus 2:11, 12. Test yourself: Why do good works is it a means to earn Salvation or a motive to glorify The Lord Jesus?

What did Jesus Christ accomplish on that Cross?

To whom was redemption given?

Can it ever be reversed?

Chapter Seven

Guilt and Shame

Ezra 9:6,7

Psalms 51

Traumatized people chronically feel unsafe inside their bodies. The past is alive in the form of nagging interior discomfort. Their bodies are constantly bombard by visceral warning signs, and in attempt to control these processes, they often become expert at ignoring their gut feelings and in numbering awareness of what is played out inside. They learn to hide from their true selves.

Your body keeps the Score

And you are as sick as your secret

Guilt comes first

And the cousin to guilt is shame:

Shame is a cancer of the soul and if not dealt with it can destroy your soul.

You feel guilt because of something you DID

You feel shame because of something you ARE

Shame attacks your identity

God can use quilt to help put us in and work on the inside to build a relationship with Him through the gospel of Christ Jesus in forgiveness and restore us-

Self talk can led us to destruction such as...

I'll be worthy if_____

I will better myself if I gain Position, Power and Praise.

What would or could make you feel worthy? Being better? Changing a behavior?

I can feel worthy if I can be accepted by others.

Only if "I" could have a different past then I would be accepted.

If people really knew my life story they would not accept me.

On these statements we believe of ourselves and hide from ourselves in shame and that destroys our identity.

Bottom down to the ROOT

Destroy the root

Build upon the right foundation (Jesus Christ the Rock).

Steps in Changing

Change is the product of process does not happen over night.

Time is involved

Learning new and better ways in Thinking, perceiving and expressing the behavior

Change takes time

To learn new ways

Put to practice

Suffering-

One must become aware of the discomfort or dissatisfaction of the way life is going.

When one admits the need to change the progress begins

How we think

How can I change?

No one changes until the self understands the suffering in for a need to change.

The change comes in the form of

Physical change

Social change

Spiritual change

The emotional change

Humility must come before one admits the need for change and seeks help.

God does not want you to dwell in your shame. Follow these four steps to embrace freedom:

1. Dare to draw near to God. (Hebrews 10:22)
2. Know that your past sin is gone for good (Micah 7:19) and that there is no condemnation for you as a child of God. (Romans 8:1)

3. Through good counsel from friends and loved ones, intentionally disassociate yourself from your past. (2 Corinthians 5:17; Philippians 3:13)
4. Worship God regularly to clean your conscience. (Hebrews 10:2) Send away your shame. Actively trust in God for your healing and permanent deliverance from the past.

Chapter Eight

Good News Turned Bad

How well do we understand when the Good News of the Gospel turns Bad!

It is important for many to understand the connections between what we hear and how we perceive about God. Inwardly we all have a mental picture of God. That is our perception of what God is in His Character. This comes about with what we have either experienced in the past, those haunting memories, or what teaching about God we were taught. The most determinative factor is the personal feelings of who God really is. Is He a loving, caring, compassionate Father or a Judge ready to declare a sentence upon you of doom? Many with a genuine heart led spirit are caught up into an inner conflict between what we know about God and how they feel towards Him.

Something to think about here:

Reality is nothing more than the passing of the present time of the circumstance that we are present engaged in for the moment. Moreover, that reality can be perceive from the lens of our understanding that we interpret this situation as being right or wrong, good or evil. All things present through lens in which we view are reality to us; but not all things is interpreted to what they are in actuality are. We only perceive them to be good or bad by our interpretation and that is usually from experiences. God is true in reality but how you perceive or interpret Him is from past teachings.

Because of guilty feelings or emotions, we draw away from a loving Father, rather than allowing Him, to give us freely the salvation that is through Christ Jesus. Our head theology is excellent for as perceiving God is Holy, Righteous and separated from sinners. However, thanks be unto our Lord Jesus Christ through the shedding of His blood has brought salvation unto as many as will call upon Him.

John 1:12 But as many as received him, to them gave he power to become the sons of God, *even* to them that believe on his name:

Because God is Holy it is perceive in our past experiences and guilt and we run from God rather unto God to ask mercy. This begin back in Genesis 3

Genesis 3:8 And they heard the voice of the LORD God walking in the garden in the cool of the day: and Adam and his wife hid themselves from the presence of the LORD God amongst the trees of the garden.

Gen 3:9 And the LORD God called unto Adam, and said unto him, Where *art* thou?

Gen 3:10 And he said, I heard thy voice in the garden, and **I was afraid**, because I *was* naked; and I hid myself.

Gen 3:11 And he said, Who told thee that thou *wast* naked? Hast thou eaten of the tree, whereof I commanded thee that thou shouldest not eat?

Here is the fact: God has never turned His back on man; but we run from Him because of fear; failure, frustrated not being able to live up to the demands that God has required.

John 3:16 For God so loved the world. Herein lays the fact; even though Adam sinned against God, and even though Adam suffer the consequences of sinning; God still came down to fellowship with him. But Adam and Eve hid themselves in fear. Healing of the inner soul can only come through a heart-felt repentance and faith in God. To understand God loves them despite the sin. God truly loves us just the way we are, for He knows the heart of man even in the fallen state and

God's unconditional love is reaching out but man still in rejecting of this offer.

The fact is God does not wait until we perfect ourselves, or do better but He alone took the first step in sending His only Son into the world to become sin that we might become the righteousness of God.

2Corintians 5:17 Therefore if any man *be* in Christ, *he is* a new creature: old things are passed away; behold, all things are become new.

2Co 5:18 And all things *are* of God, who hath reconciled us to himself by Jesus Christ, and hath given to us the ministry of reconciliation;

2Co 5:19 To wit, that God was in Christ, reconciling the world unto himself, not imputing their trespasses unto them; and hath committed unto us the word of reconciliation.

2Co 5:20 Now then we are ambassadors for Christ, as though God did beseech *you* by us: we pray *you* in Christ's stead, be ye reconciled to God.

2Co 5:21 **For he hath made him *to be* sin for us, who knew no sin; that we might be made the righteousness of God in him**.

Can we improve on what God has done?

If Christ Jesus became sin for us, bore our sins; taken them away from us and took them to the cross; died for us that we might become the righteousness of God can we add anything to that?

Fact is; God did not wait until we got better, but while we were without strength in due time Christ died for the ungodly (Romans 5:6). This unconditional love (the agape) of God is seen throughout Scriptures. Because of the Cross of Christ, because of that "so great of salvation" (Hebrews 2:3) we have not received the spirit of bondage again to **fear;** but you have received the Spirit of adoption (position of belongingness and worth), whereby we cry, Abba, Father (Romans 8:15). God who knows our end from the beginning thereby knows humans will fail, we are failures, sinners and man at his best state is vanity (Psalms 39:5). It is already been declared in the hands of God's Word "all our righteousness is nothing but as filthy rags" (Isaiah 64:6).

How does the gospel of good news is turn around into bad news. Because of twisted Scriptures that we interpreted. Taking the word out of context that affects our feelings or concepts of God. It is because what people hear can be very different from what one might have actually said.

Example

John 11:11 These things said he: and after that he saith unto them, Our friend Lazarus sleepeth; but I go, that I may awake him out of sleep.

Joh 11:12 Then said his disciples, Lord, if he sleep, he shall do well.

Joh 11:13 **Howbeit Jesus spake of his death: but they thought that he had spoken of taking of rest in sleep.**

Joh 11:14 Then said Jesus unto them plainly, Lazarus is dead.

Joh 11:15 And I am glad for your sakes that I was not there, to the intent ye may believe; nevertheless let us go unto him.

Joh 11:16 Then said Thomas, which is called Didymus, unto his fellowdisciples, **Let us also go, that we may die with him.**

Act 8:30 And Philip ran thither to *him,* and heard him read the prophet Esaias, and said, Understandest thou what thou readest?

What is spoken and how we hear what is spoken is important. To the Hindu the term "born again" from the Bible means a belief system of reincarnation and a cycle of rebirths in this nature body until one finds salvation (release) from the cycle.

Our concepts are composed from mental pictures made up from many pieces of a puzzle, which come from many sources. For example, Home to one with a loving family that word would describe "Heaven" or a rest haven; to one that is abused, rejected, unwanted that word "Home" describes "Hell".

Our concepts of God are from life lived experiences, interpersonal relationships, and the teachings we were given. The things we have been taught are more important than what we can learn. Past perceptions about God are so embedded into our mentality, which can affect our ideas about God.

While it is Biblically correct that the Holy Spirit is the One that illuminates the truth found in God's Word, what the listener hears and pictures and even feels has to be filtered through them. God can not nor will not break man's will. God does not remove nor does He by pass the personality by which a person perceives things. Galatians 2:20

I am crucified with Christ: **nevertheless I live**; yet not I, but Christ liveth in me: and the life which I now live in the flesh I live by the faith of the Son of God, who loved me, and gave himself for me.

It is important to note the phrase found "**nevertheless I live**". Even though one has been born again, saved, sealed until the day of redemption, the unique character of the "I still live"; it is our design, character and personalities that will remain in the: "I live".

How the truth is interpreted depends on the individual perception of things revealed. But when those perceiving receptors have been damaged, the Biblical truths get distorted or twisted. Even to the best, devoted Christian clarifying their concepts of God is a life long task and central part of reaching maturity in Christ.

> John 1:14 And the Word was made flesh, and dwelt among us, (and we beheld his glory, the glory as of the only begotten of the Father,) full of grace and truth.

God had gone as far as He would in types and shadows of the Old Testament and speaking through the prophets; but these had become to subjection of distortions of sinful and damaged hearers. Only when the Word became flesh (human life) was it possible to fully understand a true picture of God "full of grace and truth".

But the interpretation of those words in the Bible remain distorted by the influenced of our past beliefs and relationships with our perception of God. While it is true "the fear of the Lord is the beginning" it is not the end. Psalms 33:8 "Let all the earth fear the LORD: let all the inhabitants of the world stand in awe of him."

> And Psalms 33:18 "Behold, the eye of the LORD *is* upon them that fear him, upon them that hope in his mercy;"

Many have a distorted perception of God. As how they think, God feels towards them. Often some will believe "God doesn't really care or is concerned about them as individuals."

Some are not sure that He cares if they exist or not because of God's permissive will is being carried out. (*another subject). Some think God is mean, like a tyranny God who is never please and holds unforgiving marks against them, holds grudges, and constantly reminding them of their sins. Like a Judge ready to past sentence or a Santa Claus who makes a list and checks it twice. Judging our performance how well we do or measuring up. Some have the perception of God as a huge eye watching everything we do, waiting to catch them at some failure or wrongdoing. A Judge holds the Ten Commandments and ready to strike us down if we even think about breaking one of them. Many instead of trusting God is predictable in His steadfastness and responsibility in His faithfulness, many loving Christians are filled with fears and anxiety because at a gut-level they sense God to be untrustworthy that He is willing to save you this moment but if you fail to live up to the "Christian Life" out you go. The bottom line is an in and out salvation. Yes we are willing to accept salvation through repentance and faith and the cross seems as a down payment but God hands you the payment book. They sing the song amazing grace but in a fear of a performance level, they live fearful of God who is willing to accept them in love mercy and grace through our Lord and Savior Jesus Christ. The Christian in general sense God only accepts them on a Conditional Method, measuring up on "good works".

Their life becomes like those people that deal with paranoia but theirs is a spiritual one. These people can take the most loving, affirming statements and interpret them as insults and rejections. Christians with damaged love receptions can rake the good news and turn it into bad as they consistently select the Scriptures that speaks of wrath, punishment, judgment and lets not forget the unpardonable sin to increase the guilt feeling, condemnation and judging others to lift them up as a deeper revelation of knowing God; by passing a loving Father. Unless Christian teachers truly understand the text and context of which the text is drawn, they will not be able to free those with damaged perceptions about God. Instead they will actually harm those and add more guilt driving force to separate themselves from God even farther.

> Romans 2:4 Or despisest thou the riches of his goodness and forbearance and longsuffering; not knowing that the goodness of God leadeth thee to repentance?

The fact that we may have been victims of painful experiences and hurtful relationships does not excuse us from responsibility. While there are factors in life that we did not choose nor have control over, including our fallen nature through Adam; but these facts remain and produce distorted mental perceptions of God. There are facts in our personal life that we neither choose nor control such as our biological and psychological inheritance, our geographical location, the environment of which we were born, our parents, the accidents we have experienced, birth defects and the tragedies or traumas we face. It is these things that remind us because sin enter the world God is in control but under the permissive will in His dealings now and that will change. The same gravity that binds us to earth can also kill us if we fall out of a two-story building. This permissive will does not change God's love towards us.

These un-chosen events make up what the Scriptures would term our infirmities. Infirmities are the weakness of this flesh, the crippling defects of the body, mind and spirit. While these are not "the sins" but are qualities of our personalities, which predispose us and incline us toward certain fleshy desires, these are the triggers points that we are weak in our defense that undermine our resistance to temptation and sin.

On the opposite side of the coin and where we are responsible. Some have chosen to make wrong responses to God and to other people. Some have continued to hold on unto resentments, bitterness, and have chosen deliberately to disobey God because of feelings of a victim rather than a victor in Christ Jesus. Because of this attitude, those who practice these things must accept the consequences. We as individuals need to forgive much; but we also stand in need of forgiveness. There is a need in forgiving one another; even as Christ has forgiven us. There is a deep need within the circle of Christians for forgiveness. We must learn to forgive others and that is the key to unlock the greater that is the need to forgive ourselves. Forgiving ourselves sets us at liberty from the bondage of guilt. As we pray to ask God to forgive us that also includes forgiving ourselves as victims and begin to live in victory. This kind of full forgiveness is found in the Epistles of the New Testament in the love of God, through and in the Lord Jesus Christ. Until we accept this fact we will never experience lasting "righteousness, peace and joy in the Holy Spirit" Romans 14:17 We are no longer are "slaves" but friends with God through and in Christ Jesus (John 15:15).

> **Matthew 11:28-30 Comeunto me**, all *ye* that labour and are heavy laden, and I will give you rest. Take my yoke upon you, and learn of me; for I am meek and lowly in heart: and ye shall find rest unto your souls.

> For my yoke *is* easy, and my burden is light.

God I can't live the Christian life. I struggle each and everyday. I truly love you and thank you for all the things you did for me. Trying to live the life of a Christian is hard as I battle with this flesh having the guilt, rejection and sense of belonging back with you. I have become the victim of hurtful memories of the past experiences in church as I fail to live up to what is require all I can do is bow my knee unto you as King and ask for mercy. And praise God I found another that step up and said Father; forgive them they know not what they do. And this very one that hung on the cross that shed His blood has taken me in His arms to lead me all the way. No longer is the Christian life a struggle because He (Jesus) lives and because He gave His all in love for me that alone drives me back to you God and even though I think I'm a failure in your Word I see I can do all things through Christ which strengthens me. Amen it is a settled issue with you God because your Son has reconciled us back to you. Salvation you brought forth is a gift and God thank you for so great a gift. Amen and Amen!

This friend settles the battle between the struggle between the flesh and the Spirit. While in this flesh can come no good thing outside Christ Jesus in you the hope of glory; yet in your spirit we can have peace with God not looking unto ourselves but unto the author and finisher of our faith.

Printed in the United States
By Bookmasters